The Idiot's Calendar

Poems by Raphael P. Maurice

Kansas City Spartan Press Missouri

Spartan Press
Kansas City, Missouri
spartanpresskc.com

Spartan Press

Copyright (c) Raphael P. Maurice, 2018
First Edition 1 3 5 7 9 10 8 6 4 2
ISBN: 978-1-946642-36-3
LCCN: 2017964224

Design, edits and layout: Jason Ryberg
Author photo: Raphael Maurice
Cover image and design: Michael Keth
All rights reserved. No part of this publication may be
reproduced or transmitted in any form or by any means,
electronic or mechanical, including photocopying,
recording or by info retrieval system, without prior
written permission from the author.

Spartan Press would like to thank Prospero's Books, The Fellowship of N-finite Jest, The Prospero Institute of Disquieted P/o/e/t/i/c/s, Will Leathem, Tom Wayne, Jeanette Powers, j.d.tulloch, Jason Preu, Mark McClane, Tony Hayden and the whole Osage Arts Community.

Some of these poems have appeared in *Vending Machine Press, U City Review, Piecrust, Sou'Wester,* and other fine publications. My thanks to my dedicated, patient and brilliant family, without whom these efforts seem wasted. I would also like to thank Ann Daniels, Joshua Kryah, Allison Funk, Andrew Cox, and many others I have forgotten to mention here.

CONTENTS

[Idiot's Passport] / 1

[An Idiot's Sonnet by the Sea] / 3

[A History Here] / 4

[Schoolyard] / 5

[Rectitude] / 6

[An Evening with You] / 7

[Victories] / 9

[Gas Station in Gerald] / 10

[Hippolytus] / 11

[My Better Life in the Country] / 12

[The Storm] / 14

[His Dream] / 15

[Utopia] / 16

[The Natural Order] / 18

[This Land Is Your Land] / 20

[Lao Tzu / Roy Orbison] / 21

[For James Wright] / 23

[Patience] / 24

[The Idiot's Calendar] / 25

[Fragments of Heraclitus: Translated in Gerald, Missouri] / 26

[Κοφα, or The Daughter] / 32

[Sonnets of Heraclitus: From Ephesus to Gerald]

[Sonnet 59] / 56

[Sonnet 61] / 57

[Sonnet 76] / 58

[Sonnet 78] / 59

[Last Poems]

[Charon] / 60

[Dance] / 62

[To Go To Hell For This, Love] / 64

For Jeremiah Driver

[Idiot's Passport]

They gave us passports to a newer world -
We landed safely, pills and food stamps in our pockets.
The officials stamped our papers,
and the red stamp bore the word, idiot.
Somewhere between there and hell,
I called out to my brothers and sisters.

But they did not hear, my brothers and sisters,
thrown too hard into the world,
this place that like a flower unfolds its hell,
reeking petals stuffed into our pockets.
For we are all of us, gorgeous idiots.
You've only to glance at these glossy papers,

a stamp bearing red ink upon our papers.
Oh, my pock-marked brothers and sisters,
you pill-fueled, laughing idiots
not quite at home in the world
of coats and socks and pockets:
and now you're much too warm for hell.

I began to fear, but not the place of hell.
I tossed onto fires my papers
after tearing at my pockets,
tearing out at my brothers and sisters,
thrown and dizzy from the world.

What exactly makes an idiot?

I think it might be us, we idiots
who have searched through hell
and the world
with red-inked passports and papers,
with little hope for our brothers and sisters.
How I would keep them in my pockets!

How you guard my secrets and my loves
in your heavy pockets.
For there is no wheelchair ramp for the idiots,
my suffering brothers and sisters
who starve in hell,
lunched upon their papers
and had little to report back to the world.

I empty out my pockets and wait in hell,
as new idiots arrive daily with their papers.
I am joyed to call my brothers and sisters
from the world.

[An Idiot's Sonnet by the Sea]

With me you walk through brutal days
both of us confined to our separate minds.
While netted, trapped within these crabbed lines,
I thought of you and those nights in which you raged.
As if you'd seen another world that collapsed & lay
at your feet in order to be sorted out by time.
It wasn't so. The errors we had made were blind,
like Homer's catalogue of ships —
undone by the ocean's play —
the sea it claps against the hull,
seawater spits out the bay.
I did not want things to pan out like this,
the hit of water against another boat,
our dreadful, waterlogged days and nights.
It was your drenched naming of each and every kiss.
You'd lean, and lip-to-lip, touch what you had hoped:
and in the drooling night you groped to find
a darker sort of bliss.

[A History Here]

My father & I walked across the dead
land of trees & scrub, land of flat stones taking their
fair due of sunlight, rain, each ghost a neighbor in the
breeze, a ghost signaling from a tree's crotch.
The canopy of jeweled leaves shivered in winds
that rattled at my heart. Somewhere, like nowhere.
A copperhead struck out at him from beneath its rock.
He raised the knife, & with a steel-toed boot,
trapped it beneath his sole, inching nearer to the crown.
As it hissed, he hacked the gasping head until
it came loose, fell. In winds that rattled through
my heart, it lay forked, still. We went on, said nothing.
Nowhere. Dropping a sandstone over it, he threw dirt
onto its grave, & scored the earth with the viperish
teeth of the survival knife. This was the spot near
creek beds where I'd cried out to a sapling ended young
with my own knife, my own hands. I'd knelt before it —
a history here — I'm sorry. I'm sorry. When my brother
came in drunk again, they went at each other in terrible
gusts & fists that rained against their bodies, faces,
the front door ruined, my mother looking out,
the window cracked near a cedar Christmas tree.
The snow's silence crept into the night as she silently
rectified the mess. Nothing was said, like a great,
dead pause in music— that space where we wait
for a god or language to explain how we wound up
as we are, here, right here.

[Schoolyard]

Were you there when they crucified my Lord?

You, you might say a few words to us,
   and prove yourself all over again.

For instance, whenever I see you in your tree,
   I ask why you don't come down.

And then I curse you. Curse your stupid name
    and then freeze and look stupidly around the yard.

What would happen if you appeared?
If you appeared to me and the other idiots,
   and stared into us.
What clever things we would say.

Like you were the school pariah, but tougher than us,
most likely we'd lie.
We would spare your feelings and say we hadn't seen
      you descend from out the tree.

Comb your hair. Walk toward us.

[Rectitude]

    The police caught me near these weeping willows
creeping up lakeside. I gave up under dawn's
wrack and ribbon. They took what little I had.

And I was long gone, babbling my season's luck
and miscarriages.
The county jail. Silent as a brick, stiller than God.

I crashed out on the bunks logic, its rectitude.
Rectitude. What a strange word for dead monks
to thrash about.

And I dreamed the horse-faced sheriff was reading
from a sacred book. His boots propped on the desk.
His words scattered by an oscillating fan.

    It was litany. It was the liturgy at my father's funeral,
reverent as the edge of morning glories, a reckoning.

It was a catalogue of tender girls I'd loved,
their terrible fates blowing against those crooked trees.

[An Evening with You]

We know the story. You are telling me how after six dragging years, the Golden Empress tree will erupt in spring with reeking blossoms.

That the world ceases being strange. In winter, against moonlight, her branches—writhe against each shadow.

I know this too well. I know the acrid taste of whiskey, and stifled feeling. The world hums. Stupidly, we stare at the Empress and cover our coughs.

I begin to tell you that I took too hard the dream of a horse flogged to death, and so dreamt later that I was swimming through sewers, bits and pieces of horses splayed and sawed within water, floating in green, unending water.

My wife awoke to my screams, caressed my hand, later we made love, we later fell asleep. But we know this. We know our own grief. It is the place in which we appear.

When I was small, you gave books that taunted and called. I would read, tearing at myself, stumbling over heavy names that are now too familiar.

I'd shred face and cover, hidden from your sight.
It was not until this year we could speak. You know
this, because I say it now. Beneath the bed I'd hide
torn paper, and hope you would not miss the tomes
you'd dolled out.

But the Empress. The Empress is true beneath the
snow, the fallout, the choruses, the verse. We know
the story. What, between love and knowledge,
will do?

You know the story. We are here, hiding from our
wives, hiding, wondering about a tree. I see their
shadows in the distant windows of the house, the
snow falling harder.

I stick out my tongue, catch a flake, and wait
for what's next.

[Victories]

Having reckoned victories,
I've only once been right.
On the ride home from school,
as certain as a basic sum,
certain as the sun's blameless geometry,
sunning the green, vinyl seat, warming it—
my mother is in the yard,
waving, shouting at the neighbors.

[Gas Station in Gerald]

Yesterday, my father saw me for the first time.
We were in his Impala, and my hands were fumbling
for a cigarette.

Here, he said. *Take the money.*
His eyes were broken, twisted, the way lightning is
against the open dead skies of Gerald, Missouri.

I can't. I just can't.

I don't know why we had stopped, but we had.
I remembered the pencil box he'd bought me
on my first day at school.
Thinking of it—the color of old blood,
the wood worn smooth—thinking of it,
I want to bring him closer to me.

My God. Those years in the ward, he said
in Gerald, Missouri.
My God.

[Hippolytus]

I came to tell you of the horses
gathered like hulls and stirring in the fields.
We fed them sugar and carrots,
then pursued and shamed our bodies in the creeks.
Suddenly, these creatures wade in pools of red
rippling, ribboning out of the earth,
for there is no such thing as control.
Hooves, black as blood, tell us this,
the sky singing over our heads—
you have always wanted too much.

[My Better Life in the Country]

I suppose I should tell of the things I liked here.
I liked the way hay bales looked liked giant, golden
tablets, and often I thought God would appear and
reach down, take a pill and then drink from
a water-swollen lake.

Horses. Just out the window, the fields of wheat
stirring against their great bodies, and if you approached
with carrots or apples, you would know love and fear.
You would understand, though you had not yet read
of Hippolytus drowning in magnetic surf, your own
desire to be near horses.

I would take sticks and make crosses, taping the pieces
together. And through the fields, I heard hymns
and songs, as I curled like a violin-scroll beneath a tree.
I would awake, crosses at my feet, after a good sleep
beneath an oak.

I liked the way my mother, who smelled of fresh laundry,
hung clothes on the line my father put up. I even like
to recall them bickering. She had instructed him on
how to hang the cord and where to place the poles.
And he, in his wry, southern voice: *opinions are
inexpensive, dear.*

I liked him reading from Homer at night.
I liked the way the sea, which was simply the field
with its horses and hay bales, roared and hushed me
to sleep. I would drift off with the Iliad
beneath my pillow, muttering, *father, father.*

And though it burns at times, I don't exactly regret
that later I would go mad with what he had taught me:
Greek letters on wax paper hung like ghosts from
the dormitory walls. I saw Alpha to Omega borne
into buildings that galloped at me. Useless when
a doctor muttered back, *ten-year recovery.*

Most of all, I liked the possibility of forgiveness.
I like it now. And I have always liked the way memories
have an order all their own — like a boy arranging
lettered blocks upon the steps of his parents' home,
or a mare nudging a colt, guided by a logic that
we can only witness.

[The Storm]

Wait it out   purblind   near the bales.

Sit out the deafening   song of dust   then the rain's sea

a gale   quickening   expanse of the anger-crows.

The uproar   rides the lightning-spines

furred   blue   electric   backs of hysterical horses.

Swollen coveter   crimson howl

demented   water   thief—

leave us our pile   our flood-bones.

Add up the crawling   the cowering   things of earth,

and divide   monster   divide.

[His Dream]

I.

She sits in a corner, knees pressed to her breast,
swearing that the bandage will unravel at the wrist
and turn into a dove, signaling forth the Holy Ghost.

Enter *Spiritus Sancti:* shaking foundations, shattering
barred windows, demolishing palaces of the mad.
Her pill-blood and the bituminous nights are cleansed
by the air about the ruins.

He is taking her somewhere, through an unknown city.
A bright city of flame leading to a park –
her hand in his, a second flame...

II.

Come morning, the dream-work still persists,
coloring the walls, climbing into coffee cups,
dancing through plumes of cigarette smoke.
It is as if we inhabit not two worlds, but three.
The last — we must ...
The last world is that plank we must walk between
wakefulness and sleep:

III.

She sits in a corner of the wind...

[Utopia]

This is the hard land of miracles.
Land of arias over the fields,
land of music made by the god
at morning. Land of nerves,
land of the timpani-heart, savage, struck
by the hands of the blind.
This is the land of lint & Lee jeans,
pockets outturned, begging like dogs.
This is the land of bales, of the final storm
that bares open the earth, does violence,
and, in turn, is spat upon by its own children.
This is the land of early, eager kisses.
This is the overturned log — it too, part of the land —
where she offered herself
leaving chicken scratches on your heart,
the log of days & nights, the map of the rudderless
& hell-bent. This is the land of celebrations,
one boy in a party hat blowing a red kazoo.
This is the land of basement homes
where the owners fail, year after year,
to come out into the sun. This is the lonely land,
land of eminent domain, land of the open palm.
This is the land of the greeter in her wheelchair,
welcoming you to another land, fluorescent,
on the fritz, the new land of the mentholated voice,

hoarse & bitten by the Crab.
This is the land of forgiveness,
the land of good horses grown wild from neglect,
the paralytic forgives them, & so have I.
This is the land where our visions go bucking,
land of stirring and beginnings, land of the sunset.
This is the land of justice,
though no land is. This is the land of sincerity &
toothache, old eyes searching for a daughter,
noses rubbed clean off at the bar.
This is the land of ditches, land of the dogs' grave,
land from which you can never go back,
return, land of the pillow that hits the hay,
of lightning that can never go home,
land of the bleak snow, of waiting at the door
with presents but never knocking. This is the place
we were ashamed of, that seems now like so many
others, its size & scale reliant on the mind's weather,
land of the unmapped, land of my dreams.

[The Natural Order]

It was the time the wicker sofa flew down a ravine.
During rains when my father stole into the shadows
along a highway where the rigs screamed.
A buck-fifty, soaking wet.

It's time to make accountings of what's been seen.
To hope what was seen can be recalled.

To pray for an aerial view, a plotted grid of green (why?),
a garden-patch, the eye's strength, the sure-shot bee-bee
kept (still inside the knee)

as a reminder that your first love was God.

God came and shot you in the knee, point blank.
It was in a pasture where, from time to time,
motorcycles went by like bumble-bees.
God was a boy then, laughing with fire in his hair,
begging no word of it to His mother.

Over the hill the ballplayers came
and took the field. As you pitched,
the lower leg of your uniform was veined with blood.
Sodas all around, the fizz of sugar in your face—
victory.

When Dr. Johnson (sincerely came) and tried
to pry it out, it didn't come. The middle of town,
brown vinyl and zipped up building,
sun singing against the day.

Then rain came again and you were big in love.
The way it must be, skipping through a kerosene-town,
poking around the right knee, staring at the field
of green and gold, the wind-scorched dream.

He'd rarely bought ice cream.
But there were so many books to read.
Enough always to digest and wait on.

And the forest was heavy and dark.
It was an amusement park into which not even God
could go. His wrong height, wrong hair, wrong—
and so rejected from the ride.

You kept this love mute within your chest.
When the rains abandoned Gerald,
you took his hand, his life, his side.

[This Land Is Your Land]

After an afternoon driving through
where I grew up — Viper's Lane,
Retirement Road, Holy Family Hill
buried beneath snow,
the hill dotted by black, electric birds,
blurred by sun, dotted by meth —
shacks, near the ditch of dead pups,
places I'd abandoned — and I lie and tell you
that nothing much happened,
nothing like Bobby Hoffman,
the cows masticating, dumb, dumb, dumb,
entering into bruise-colored barns,
a farmer's sudden wave, church suppers
where most went hungry for the Ghost — I am
still here, cold and raving,
eager to tear and torch the leaning
porches, all they seem to mean —
you tell me to calm down. (A day later,
over morning coffee, you'll tell your mother
on the phone you're sad, sad, and might need
a prescription for meds, or impossible,
a vacation far from our histories, an island, Lexapropolis,
something, one true love.) But now I get out
of the car to smoke, onto the green shoulder,
looking out over the plots and grids
of Gerald, suddenly, breathing the raw air.

[Lao Tzu / Roy Orbison]

On a black road I
burned a copy of the Tao,
your favorite book.

Before the fire,
you were betrayed & sickened,
you left me crying …

Crying over you.
And so I will always be
crying over you …

Forgive the river,
the trees are quite terrible
and you keep yelling

pedigrees & such.
Woman, whose daughter were you?
I cannot name this …

With sunglasses on,
I sing for the drowned & damned,
fumbling for words,

my shoe polish hair,
obscure as my Chevrolet,
'57— flat black —

begging the question,
what to croon about now, dear,
near my escape route?

[For James Wright]

Miles down the locust road towards town,
at the dusty bar in which years later I will waste
myself on an unhinged, three-year bender—
material for a few fractured songs—
they smoked and drank, the men's speech
turning into the rhetoric of locusts.

With heavy lungs and desiccated throats,
the old voices teem and mutter in my skull,
shames that cut and bore
like saws and splitters, a mill of failure
churning at the river's shore.

The reeking water still summons us back to work.

[Patience]

The old man is twisted again,
reeling around the house,
popping his leather belt.
A boy waits near the road.
He can hear locusts.
Somehow, they are.
Somehow they are everywhere.

[The Idiot's Calendar]

According to the Idiot's Calendar,
it's been days since I've heard a voice.
Winter devours the trees.

Past creek beds and shacks,
there is a girl living near the fields,
in her father's house— a grieving place.
She is out there,
beyond the frozen stalks and ditches.

Now, snow falls.
From this window,
I call out with all of my body.

A fence post is abandoned by a crow.
Let it carry some of myself to her,
a voice, somehow, my own.

Like the figure of her carrying the father through fires,
something as impossible as a city must occur.
Quickly. According to the Idiot's Calendar,
it's been days.

[Fragments of Heraclitus: Translated in Gerald, Missouri]

61

The sea's water is both pure & filthy:

Fish drink it, and they are sustained.

For men, the water is undrinkable, lethal.

59

Curved, but straight:

That is the path, the way of writing.

64

The thunderbolt steers the sum of all things.

13

Pigs adore filth,

but not fresh water.

32

One thing, the most brilliant thing,

allows and disallows itself

to be called the god.

78

The human condition is to misunderstand.

The god has kept all understanding.

82

The most handsome ape

cannot compare to the beauty

of the ugliest among us.

87

Behold that moron, worked into

a frenzy by *anything* he might hear.

93

The oracle at Delphi doesn't reveal

or conceal answers: It merely gives

a sign.

97

Dogs bark.

They bark at anyone

unknown.

107

The stupid & barbaric soul

is one that relies

on stupid and barbaric hearsay.

95

Stupidity is best kept close to the chest.

108

So many reckonings, books, learning:

none of it leads to wisdom of any sort.

78

The drunkard's soul is wet. So that

he stumbles along while a beardless boy

must guide him, it, that … the blinded drunk.

96

Shit is somewhat better

than a corpse.

89

For the ones who are Awake,

there is a common world.

Sleep brings privacy, sequestering

us into private places.

85

Because passion

tells us to do so,

we ransom our souls on the cheap.

42

Throw out (it's your right)

Homer from the book of names—

thrash him. Archilochus, too.

72

What is closest to us is the furthest of things.

22

Dig tons of dirt,

unearth an ounce of silver.

21

We see death once we are awake—

sleep considers the things we see

while we are sleeping.

12

Stepping into the same river,

we are touched by radically different waters.

[Κοφα, or The Daughter]

Dramatis Personae:
Audrey, Kora, Miss, Daughter: played by me
Samuel Becket: played by himself
Dalmatians: played by pleasant dogs
The Speaker: played by libraries
Nurses & Doctors: played by history
War: played by some & not others
The Ambulance: played by a red song
Daimons: played by musicians

I.

Who remains to confabulate, to gossip —
but God — who pardons Miss Audrey
with old, rejuvenated speech?
Who pardons her from the howling desert,
frees her from the snares of teeth.
Opens her, then, as a journal, peer-reviewed,
& fiercely blows her out into the world.
We are letters arranged on varied days,
& kept unified in sweaters, pants, socks —
alphabets of loosening tongues tamped,
staked into speech, into style:
She'd scratch her body until it marked
& bled. The start of the red song that breaks
away, a tributary-sound in search of origins.

II.

Nights arrive with glinting teeth.
In dog days, I stand & sway beneath
Sirius, touching lace — a black tree — parted
ten thousand times by moonlight.
My hands grace the barred windows.
Let them havoc me.
Allow that sea of light to ribbon inward.

III.

Once, I had money (fistfuls, accounted for)
& destiny, a will. Sea-blown, Dalmatians
barked & yawned near our waterside bungalow.
Hide her & them & this
in blue sand. Hide the red beach ball
from the sun's vigilant, torn-out eye.

IV.

I have, Miss Audrey, an imagination —
drowning in ink, undone by influence.
A cot, a blanket, weak coffee.
I am a whimper rinsing up the pane.
Now, this 4th strange hymn — too late an offering —
a window-prayer to claim you back.
Who slaughters the lamb
& petitions the slackening body.

V.

Hey, Miss. It's achingly simple:
I have missed it all. Don't outwear your jacket's
welcome or shrivel in lock & key.
I raise my head to the tune of wheels,
(I am only able to raise my head, see) & down
the corridor we go — I see you
as my wayward, golden-haired daughter.
Our heads are full of static, snow.

VI.

[Samuel Beckett]

At least be Antigone.
Observe the pieties,
this place, this rest-home.
Bury me as I have buried you.
Tell the state to screw itself.
Read your ass off & dust the shelves.
Take care to fail better & again & again.
Miss, I've seen you all too well.
Don't let them banish what's good in you.
Don't let them touch right there.

VII.

A yellow tongue from the checker's mouth.
Check.
A waiter's garbled speech.
Check.
Frozen with hunger,
frozen with indecision.
Check please.
I go running hungry through
rain-slick streets, dragging,
dragging this great belly.

VIII.

When rounds are made,
a doctor hands me a cup of pills,
& jumps back. I will be jacketed.
I pull a band from a pocket,
my wedding ring for you, ma chérie.
They suddenly pounce, mistaking its flash
for a knife. We all slip in capsules & water.
Riot.

IX.

One day, Miss, I will let you truly hear
what it is I think of war.

X.

You have a weird sister, Miss.
She calls to me with her short skirts & all
that breeze — playground-torn,
I can't help but gaze.
For a minute, there is the patch of white
peering out. It is a flag, my flag,
a private, torturous view.
She climbs the jungle gym.
She climbs through the air.
I look & fuss.
I didn't want to admit this —
but here — it's somewhat new.
This is the bathroom they've given us.

XI.

Just out the window, so many confessions
to make to the birds & rain, the crow's sea.
Tell the plain truth, the behaviorist truth,
drumming knuckles against the frozen table —
a doctor scans me with his icy gaze.

XII.

And here is the cage in which I sing,
Miss, and bark at your sister,
her fucked-out eyes,
rolling back & back again.

XIII.

You & I sit on the teeter-totter.
Bright & cold morning,
church hymns spill from hills.
 I fall from the top, opening my head,
as pigeons gather around my body.
You spring again from my mind:
My daimon can outdo your daimon.

XIV.

So the docs ask me to tell them how she came to be.
- from these songs .
- from the long days spent quiet, alone.
- from nous, Plotinus, and the sheet of stars.
- from really knowing things, not just kind of.
- a sister, who will be free as well.
- from the private realm, now public as a library.
Audrey, you always had access to these vaults.
Undo the lock & let the stars sling low.
Mr. Roethke learned by going
where he had to go.

XV.

Once, there was a ride in an ambulance,
& it cried & sang out & bled over the highways
& I raised up
& looked out the back window
& said how wonderful it all was ,
that we were headed to the city
where you & I could see a baseball game.

XVI.

Popcorn?

XVII.

Evening drops with the quickness of grasshoppers
flicking around the field near a movie theater.
My date & I enter the row of heads
& faces tuned to the screen.
It sounds like rain.
I think of you, Audrey,
as what's-her-name will not touch nor be touched.
A boy whom I have wanted to punch out,
 have kicked to dust in my more savage dreams,
gathers her in his flat black demon-car.
& I can't remember who was in the movie —
Yes. I remember.
I walked home, groping & feeling up the wind.
It received me.
But I wanted your small hands to pluck tickets —
flowers — waiting near the ball diamond.

XVIII.

This is what I think of war.

XIX.

Daimon.
Where do they send us
when we are stricken, struck out,
our mental passports stamped?
Glinting teeth clenched,
Sirius barking,
Audrey yelling off her head,
it being days since this?
I hardly know.
I know that I do not.

XX.

Here is a dead dog out the window.
The grasses stir, announcing an end.
This is portrait of this artist as a dog.
They must have shot him good,
right in the arm. Redder than red.
Where they should.

XXI.

I continue free to make & remake you, Audrey.
I am the great community sculptor.
This is where I, all of us, work.
We toil about plastic flowers
& loose our powers in a shout of rain.

XXII.

Come along now. Alone. With five dollar words.
You are a palimpsest
coating the walls here. Here,
these hands are fierce with nerves,
the fiercest harp — & shaking,
hold photographs of you then & now —
A nurse asks what I am looking at.
I stare down at these medicated paws.

XXIII.

I was merely looking, ma'am, at this —
the girl in plaid, small,
petting a Dalmatian by the shore.
A puppy licking an older woman's face,
grace falling sunlit out her hair.

XXIV.

Would you hold this book?

XXV.

Grandma called her *that fat girl,*
who ordered pizza & phoned us in the ward.
She asked when I'd be freed as I heard
the shackle's plastic teeth, tisk, tisk.
Oh, Grandma — Audrey has gained weight, it's true.
How's are the baseball games & how's the story?
Is your husband still bald?
Most importantly, how are you?

XXVI.

The days are numbered here.
Kora does not peer through the clouds.
My moods settle down as I have lied to the doctors,
& have made great friends,
comrades, too, who have made
many things in the communal area.
I'll be set free in a week or so.
Χαίρε, daughter.

XXVII.

I come out over the hills again.
Everything's on fire
& I cry out like a frightened choir.
What to do with all of this air & freedom?
Behind me white buildings shake.
Shadows fly out the barred windows.
There is something still inside me,
something no one will touch.
Χαίρε.

[Sonnets of Heraclitus: From Ephesus to Gerald]

[Sonnet 59]

Go, idiot. Roughen what was straight, calm.
Roughen your little poems.
We weren't put here on the threatening lands to please,
not even ourselves.

Forget the agora's madness, its night-shrieks.
Write yourself into your corner,
back into the black corner,
crooked, fenced-in. Pray off the most sacred thing,
which will and will not be called God.

Weep (like me) into your trembling hands,
weep into the mask around your face and throat.
You're the saddest s.o.b. in the cosmos.
But, that is the way we write.
This is the path we must take.

[Sonnet 61]

I'm your jitterbug boy.
I've got all the money.
I bought up all the tobacco in Honduras.
Where the water's filthy,
where fish cough up other fish.
They sustain themselves this way.

I dragged my half-corpse to the water.
I looked out and wanted to drink the surf.
I nearly Van Goughed the breakers coming in and in.
I did.

The water there was lethal.
Without an open mouth prepared to speak,
I could not sing truthfully about the sea.
I could not tell my lies so that they'd be believed.

[Sonnet 76]

I grew as ugly as an ape.
I paced this crag — a type of cage —
hoping an olive tree would tether me down,
away from the ocean's gritted teeth.

Calling out to you,
I asked what happened to our ties, once tight
as a well-strung bow.
We yelled from phone-to-phoneme,
from Ephesus to Gerald,
pacing out our treads, tearing at our hair.

If you see the sea and signal fires,
if you spot where I could be along the rocks,
then you will know.

The prettiest ape does not compare
to the ugliest soul hovering around us.

[Sonnet 78]

In stillness I grope. I search and wait.
During the dawn as the passing day has shrunk,
I feel a mystery lift.

Emptiness of half-heartedness, a frayed rope
between yes or no. Often my head tapped by something.
My sense is that it is good.

I believe it is good, humble, imperfect, embarrassed.

Tapping. Glowing. Refusing to be named.
I cannot believe or not believe.
I sit in the wind-struck orchard here,
unsure what hits, strikes, what sings, what ends.

Gentle hands through my hair.
When all has been reduced to shrugs or knowledge,
I feel the unnamable humming in my ears.

[Last Poems]

[Charon]

I ask not in sorrow,
but in wonder.
>   -- Milosz

There is a need to talk to the river-
ghosts at dusk, ask them

what is left to make here,
here, of this life, that recedes—

a harsh landscape
you were never a part of.

I roam wildly the grey
street through the tree's groans

whittled down by hard winds.
Nearing the dead waters,

I ask in sorrow, wife.
What has been, how many crack-ups,

& where have we ended up?
A heron breaks from its rookery,

silent shadow of prehistory.
It leaves traces of its young.

You were once ten-thousand suns exhumed
from the earth each morning,

as we, too, left behind our traces. Dead
skin, photographs mixed with our debts,

our children ferried back & forth
across the land, the waters. *Come,* they say.

Into the windows of my heart, *Come*—
they whisper their irretrievable sounds.

[Dance]

My wife tears her hair
as if to pull out some memory
as if to look pretty enough
to dance for me
this dance is death
the gun is near the record player
the music is humming
she need only reach
down
and dance again
across bucking floors beneath the stars
she is hungry for a new life
anyway
and I am not here to tell you this
I am not even in the room
in which she dances
I light a cigarette
and tell her that even before we die
even if at our own hands
we must be good
we must behave ourselves
even though our cells
are in revolt
and the last of the money coughs
up blood

and her hands tremble
and my arm is sore from smashing
what I wish was a body,
crumpling the great trashcan
that I wish was someone
so tonight
she sleeps after some pills
next to me
and I am certain that something has been
shattered
knowing I will not sleep
knowing something fractured
as the record keeps skipping
each time she shifts near me
in our frozen marriage bed.

[To Go To Hell For This, Love]

At that greatest of all spectacles, that last and eternal judgment, how shall I admire, how laugh, how rejoice, how exult, when I behold so many proud monarchs groaning in the lowest abyss of darkness; so many magistrates liquefying in fiercer flames than they ever kindled against the Christians; so many sages, philosophers, blushing in red-hot fires with their deluded pupils; so many tragedians more tuneful in the expression of their own sufferings; so many dancers tripping more nimbly from anguish then ever before from applause.

- Tertullian

As you lay across a fallen oak, I grew
grateful, like many heartsick boys, to God.
To my wizard who made this scene—
the forest, the jewel-birds singing in rows,
an owl's green erudition haunting its perch.
O, the ease when you, the dream, leapt into my lap.
Your body an electric map,
all for our roaming. Though some virgin-ghost does
peer into our hell, & crosses out our country names—
I was in love, & claimed that right.

Now, more than I care to mention, sleepless,
you come again to purr, though my wife's body stirs
predictably near. Missing the ease of your sunlit hair—
as I shuffle along, cleaved & wedded to the world.
In dreams I breathe god-made fumes,
lucky to sense the blaze that swallows whole.

Could you, nearest to me, measure what took place
within our choir of a forest, when we finished,
woke & let our bodies sing again?

Raphael Maurice is a poet, translator, and teacher. He resides in Washington, MO where the river keeps its secrets.

This project was made possible, in part, by generous support from the Osage Arts Community.

Osage Arts Community provides temporary time, space and support for the creation of new artistic works in a retreat format, serving creative people of all kinds — visual artists, composers, poets, fiction and nonfiction writers. Located on a 152-acre farm in an isolated rural mountainside setting in Central Missouri and bordered by ¾ of a mile of the Gasconade River, OAC provides residencies to those working alone, as well as welcoming collaborative teams, offering living space and workspace in a country environment to emerging and mid-career artists. For more information, visit us at www.oac.com

Osage Arts Community

www.ingramcontent.com/pod-product-compliance
Lightning Source LLC
Chambersburg PA
CBHW021449080526
44588CB00009B/770